Visiting the Past

The Colosseum &
the Roman Forum

Martyn Whittock

www.heinemann.co.uk/library

Visit our website to find out more information about Heinemann Library books.

To order:

☎ Phone 44 (0) 1865 888066

▤ Send a fax to 44 (0) 1865 314091

💻 Visit the Heinemann Bookshop at www.heinemann.co.uk/library to browse our catalogue and order online.

First published in Great Britain by Heinemann Library, Halley Court, Jordan Hill, Oxford OX2 8EJ, a division of Reed Educational and Professional Publishing Ltd. Heinemann is a registered trademark of Reed Educational & Professional Publishing Ltd.

OXFORD MELBOURNE AUCKLAND JOHANNESBURG BLANTYRE
GABORONE IBADAN PORTSMOUTH NH (USA) CHICAGO

Designed by Visual Image
Illustrations by Paul Bale
Originated by Ambassador Litho Ltd
Printed by Wing King Tong in Hong Kong/China

ISBN 0 431 02786 2
06 05 04 03 02
10 9 8 7 6 5 4 3 2 1

British Library Cataloguing in Publication Data

Whittock, Martyn J.
The Colosseum & the Roman Forum. – (Visiting the past)
1. Colosseum (Rome, Italy) 2. Forums, Roman – Italy – Rome – Juvenile literature 3. Rome – Antiquities – Juvenile literature
I. Title
937.6

Acknowledgements

For Louisa and Maria Bird, with love.

The publishers would like to thank Trevor Clifford for permission to reproduce all photographs.

Cover photograph reproduced with permission of Corbis.

Every effort has been made to contact copyright holders of any material reproduced in this book. Any omissions will be rectified in subsequent printings if notice is given to the Publishers.

Any words appearing in the text in bold, **like this**, are explained in the Glossary.

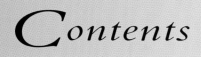

Contents

At the centre of the world

For over 600 years the Roman **Empire** grew to control land around the Mediterranean sea, in the Middle East and across much of western Europe. At the centre of this empire was the city of Rome. From here was run the greatest empire that the world had ever known. To the people living in Rome the city seemed to be at the centre of the world. At the centre of Rome itself were the Forum and the Colosseum.

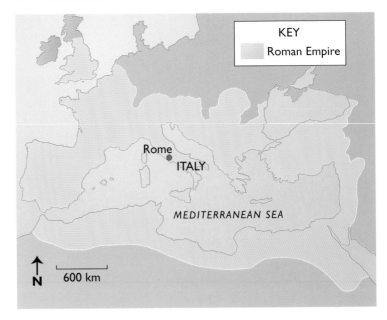

The Forum's full name was the Forum Romanum. In the Latin language of the Romans this meant the Roman Forum. But what was the Forum? It was an open space used for meetings and markets, and around it were **public buildings**. These included temples, law courts, shops and the places where the rulers of Rome met to decide how the city and the lands it controlled should be run. It was the busy, bustling, noisy and powerful centre of the growing city of Rome and its growing empire. Between the 6th century BC and 27 BC Rome was a **republic**. In this time the Forum was a very important place indeed.

The ruins of the Forum look like this today.

A new centre of Rome?

When Rome was a republic it was ruled by a group of rich **citizens** called the Senate. The Senate usually met in one of the buildings around the Forum. In 27 BC this changed, when a powerful Roman named Octavian made himself the first Roman **Emperor**. Now the Roman Empire was really ruled by one person. The Senate and its meetings became less and less important. The Forum continued to be the official centre of Rome. Great religious celebrations took place in it in honour of the many gods worshipped by the Romans. Victorious generals had their parades here. However the power was now in the hands of an Emperor. The Forum was no longer the place from which the Roman world was run.

But Emperors needed to keep the Roman people happy. Especially as these people had little say now in how the Empire was run. Emperors put on huge entertainments to please the people of Rome. In these people fought animals, people (known as gladiators) fought other people and criminals were executed in front of a crowd. In AD 80, a great new building was opened near the Forum Romanum. It was the Colosseum. In it thousands of people and animals died to keep the people of Rome entertained. It was a new centre for Rome – the greatest killing place the world had seen.

These are the ruins of the Colosseum in Rome.

Out of the marshes

In the 8th century BC, Rome was formed by uniting villages which were situated on two hills – the Palatine and Quirinal hills. Between them was a marshy valley. In about 650 BC, work began to drain this wet hollow and make it a meeting place for the settlements which had united to make Rome. Around the remains of the Forum are clues which point back to this time when it was a simple market place where once a marsh had been.

This area of the Forum is dry ground today. Romans called it the Pond of Curtius as it had previously been a swamp. Here, in Roman **legends**, a general named Curtius from the neighbouring **Sabine** tribe led an attack on the new town of Rome. He almost drowned here but his horse managed to scramble out.

When the Forum was drained of water a great drain was built called the Cloaca Maxima. At first it was an open ditch. Later it was roofed over and was used as a **sewer** for the centre of Rome. It still flows into the river Tiber.

The road which ran through the newly drained marsh was called the Via Sacra in Latin. This means the Sacred Way. It took its name from all the temples that were eventually built around the Forum. One of the earliest Roman **holy** places in the Forum was the Lacus Juturnae. This was the spring of the water goddess, Juturna, who was thought to have lived in the valley when it was a marsh.

A little shrine stood here to the goddess who was believed to look after the drain. For some reason this was Venus, goddess of love, beauty – and a sewer!

Buying and selling

The first use of the Forum was probably as a market place. On both sides of its great open space were shops called 'tabernae' in Latin. On the south side were the Tabernae Veteres (the old shops). On the north side were the Tabernae Novae (the new shops). These shops were often part of large buildings called basilicas. There were several of these around the Forum. Some of the buildings had two storeys, with meeting rooms upstairs. The central place in a basilica was the nave. Law courts often met there. In the aisles around the sides of the nave there was shelter for people to discuss business and buy and sell.

The Basilica of Constantine was finished in AD 313. Its high arches and ceilings show how large these buildings were. In the central part were law courts. Around it were places for business.

Started by Julius Caesar in 54 BC, the Basilica Julia, shows the way basilicas were built. The central space was the nave used for law courts. Round it was an arcade of two storeys containing shops. It was built on the site of the Tabernae Veteres (Old Shops).

Money, money, money ...

The Roman comedy writer Plautus wrote about different kinds of business done in the Forum. 'In the Fish Market you will find members of dining clubs. By the Old Shops you will find the money changers. There you can borrow money.' As well as these, there were bankers, barbers and butchers. In the 5th century BC, a Roman named Lucius Verginius killed his daughter with a butcher's knife in the butcher's shop in the Forum to stop her being sold as a slave. The Emperor Caligula used to stand on the roof of the Basilica Julia and throw coins into the market below to watch the shoppers fighting to get them!

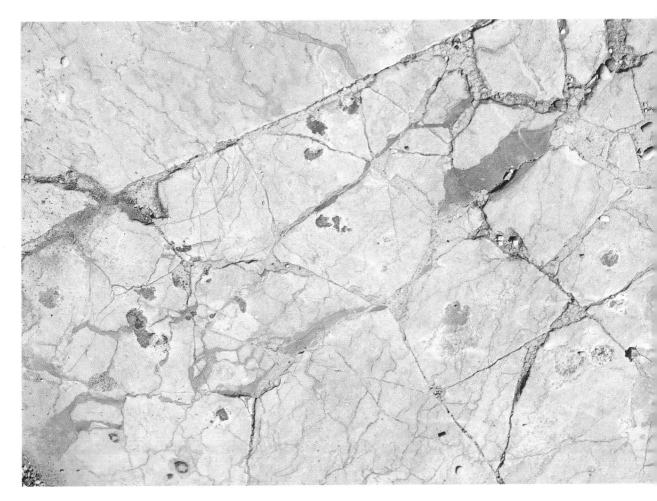

The Basilica Aemilia was burnt down twice, once in 14 BC and again in AD 410. The last time it was burnt by **barbarian Goth** tribesmen, from eastern Europe, who had captured Rome. The copper coins used by the shoppers and bankers melted into the marble floor. The green stains left by the melted coins can still be seen.

The centre of power

The Forum was the centre of Roman government while Rome was a republic (509 BC to 27 BC). One part of it, called the Comitium, was an area where **citizens** gathered to vote on new laws suggested by **magistrates**. According to **legend** this was where Romulus the founder of Rome had met the leader of the neighbouring **Sabine** tribe and made peace with him. Eventually these meetings moved out of the Forum to a larger space elsewhere in Rome, where it was easier for large crowds to gather. By the Comitium was the Rostra. This was a raised platform from which speeches could be given.

When Julius Caesar built a new Rostra he moved its position a short distance. But he kept its curved shape at the back to remind Romans of the shape of the Comitium which had been behind the original Rostra. The slots were where the **prows** of warships, captured in battle in 338 BC against another Italian tribe, were fixed as trophies. In 43 BC, the head of the murdered **politician** Cicero was stuck on one of these spikes by his enemies.

The Senate House burnt down in AD 283. It was rebuilt but later fell into ruins after the end of the Roman Empire. The building there today was built in the 1930s and is a modern **reconstruction** of the original building, started by Caesar and finished by Augustus.

The Senate

The most powerful citizens met in the Senate to discuss the government business of Rome. They often met in the temple of Castor and Pollux and made speeches from the platform in front. Powerful senators wanted people to take notice of them and support them against their rivals. The writer Cicero advised them to, 'Go down to the Forum at fixed times. Be escorted by a large crowd. It brings fame and honour.' In 44 BC building started on a new Senate House. This place, the Curia Julia, was where Senate meetings took place. When Rome became an **empire** the Senate gradually lost power because Emperors kept power for themselves, but the Forum was still officially the place from which Rome was ruled. The Emperor Galba was murdered there in AD 69 and in the same year the Emperor Vitellius was captured and executed in the Forum by his enemies.

Although emperors took power away from the Forum they did not ignore this important place. In AD 203, Emperor Septimius Severus built this great arch covered with carvings to remind Romans of his victories in battles in the Middle East.

The homes of the gods

Because the Forum was at the heart of Rome it was thought that gods lived here in **holy** places. Some of these were so old even Romans were not sure how long they had been there. There was a **sacred** fig tree whose roots were supposed to have dangled in a river here. They caught hold of the basket containing the babies Romulus and Remus who were believed to have founded Rome. Near the Lacus Curtius (Pond of Curtius) were a sacred vine and an olive tree. These were so old many Romans did not know why they were sacred. Near here was an altar to the god Vulcan and a statue of Romulus.

This is the Temple of Vesta (above), goddess of homes. It was round like an early Roman hut. In it six Vestal **Virgins** made sure a fire never went out. The name 'Vesta' comes from a Greek word meaning 'a stove'. The fire went out in AD 395 when the Christian **Emperor** Theodosius ordered the temple to be shut. As a Christian he did not believe in the pagan gods of Rome.

These ruins (left) are of the Temple of Castor and Pollux. Only the pillars from its front survive today.

Homes for the gods

Special buildings, called temples, were built where animals were **sacrificed** to the gods. In a building called the Regia lived the Pontifex Maximus, the chief priest of Rome. This was one of the oldest buildings in the Forum and had once been home to an early king of Rome before 509 BC. As well as temples of gods such as Vulcan, Saturn and Castor and Pollux, there were temples of leaders who were thought to have become gods when they died. It was believed that the gods Castor and Pollux watered their horses in the Forum after helping Romans win the battle of Regillus in 496 BC. A temple to them was built on that site in 484 BC.

Built in 29 BC the Temple of Julius Caesar treated this murdered leader as a new god. The round shape is where the altar stood, on the spot where he was **cremated** in 44 BC. Being built outside, this altar saw a change in Roman worship from private to public. This was probably to make Romans unite behind Caesar's **heir**, the first Emperor – Augustus.

Standing beside the Sacred Way, this carving shows animals about to be sacrificed to the gods. Two men, holding axes, were there to kill the animals. The animals are shown draped with flowers and ribbons because they were gifts to the gods.

Sacrifices to Roman gods were made on altars such as this one.

Justice and punishment

Criminals were tried in the Forum. Some of these courts met inside the great halls of the basilicas. Inside the Basilica Julia, 180 **magistrates** worked in four law courts. Only curtains separated the different courts. Many courts were held outside in the Forum itself. Near the Lacus Curtius was a special court where non-Romans were brought to trial. This was because Roman **citizens** had more rights than non-Roman citizens and were treated differently. In all trials 70 jurors listened to the speeches and then voted. The magistrate decided the punishments. Lawyers hired people to cheer for their side and boo the 'enemy'.

People waiting to watch a trial inside the Basilica Julia spent time playing games on boards like this one scratched into the steps outside. People found it entertaining to watch trials and they might get paid to cheer for one side or the other.

Law courts met in these arched rooms inside the Basilica of Constantine.

Prison and death

Prisoners were kept in a special prison near the Curia. It was built as two rooms, one above the other. The top room was called the Carcer. Here prisoners awaited trial. The bottom room was underground and called the Tullianum, where prisoners who were to be executed were kept. Amongst famous prisoners kept here was the **Gaullish** leader, Vercingetorix (who was later strangled) and historians believe another prisoner here was the Christian leader, St Peter (who was crucified upside down).

Crowds watched as prisoners were thrown to their deaths from the Tarpeian Rock.

Thick stone walls stopped prisoners escaping from the Carcer and Tullianum prison. There were no windows and just one door led into the Carcer.

Only a hole through the roof allowed prisoners into the underground death cell of the Tullianum. This made it impossible to escape.

Records and treasure

Rome was a well educated society. Many people could read and write and the Forum was also a place where important records were kept. These were also valuable to Roman people and their government. These records meant that decisions made by the government were documented and could be checked. Lists could be made of who owed taxes and who did which jobs. No well-run modern government could manage without its records. Roman government was very well organized.

Looking up from the Forum any passer by would have seen the building called the Tabularium. It was the Roman Public Record office. Inside its corridors and galleries were the scrolls on which important records were kept. Important documents were also kept in the Temple of Vesta. The most famous there was the **will** of Julius Caesar.

The Tabularium is next to the Forum on the edge of the hill called the Capitoline. It kept records of many of the things decided in the Forum. The upper storeys are not Roman. They were built in the 16th century by the famous Italian **sculptor** Michelangelo.

16

As safe as a bank?

Some of the temples in the Forum were also used to keep valuable objects safe. As well as the defence of the strong doors, it was believed that the gods would punish anyone who stole from there. In the **vaults** under the Temple of Castor and Pollux many rich people stored their valuable gold and silver. They could take these treasures back when they needed them. Also inside this temple were records of the weights and measures used in Rome and copies of **treaties** agreed by the Senate, engraved on bronze sheets. The government itself kept its treasure under the Temple of Saturn.

The great stone walls under the Temple of Saturn made it a very safe place for the government to keep its treasures of gold and silver. Standing there today, if you look up the hill you see the Tabularium, just behind you is the Rostra and a little to one side is the Curia where the Senate met during the Roman **Empire**. So it was a convenient place for Rome's rulers to get to.

Important documents kept inside the Temple of Vesta (left) were thought to be protected by their closeness to the fire of the goddess.

The Colosseum

The huge building called the Colosseum was started by the **Emperor** Vespasian in AD 70 and opened by his son, Titus in AD 80, with one hundred days of games. It was actually finished in AD 82. It stood three floors high and a fourth floor was added by the Emperor Alexander Severus in AD 230, making it about 48 metres high. The whole building was made to impress and entertain Roman **citizens**, who had lost a lot of their power to decide the way Rome was ruled after it became an **empire** in 27 BC. The Forum was now less important. In a way, the Colosseum had become the new centre of the Roman world. Everyone who saw it was meant to be amazed.

The 80 huge entrance arches (right) were made to hold up the outer walls and to allow a crowd of 50,000 people out in just 15 minutes! The mix of columns and arches made it very strong.

These blocks of stone (left) held great ropes which ran up to the top of the outer wall. These ropes held the edge of a great **awning** which kept the sun off people inside! Sailors from the Roman fleet worked the ropes.

Historians think over 292,000 cartloads of heavy stone blocks were used to build the Colosseum. But higher up the walls, bricks and lighter stones were used to cut down the weight being carried. These can be seen here. The stone came from quarries near Rome.

Even after the collapse of the Roman Empire in AD 410, people still tried to keep the Colosseum going. This stone records how a wealthy Roman, Decius Marius Venantius Basilius paid to rebuild it after an earthquake in AD 484. It seemed impossible to imagine Rome without its Colosseum.

These stone blocks, just below the top of the outer wall, were to support masts which held up the great awning.

In the arena

The Colosseum is a great oval shape. It is 188 metres long and 156 metres wide. It is as big as a modern international sports stadium. Its floor was made of wooden planks. These were covered in fine sand. This was brought from Egypt and was there to soak up the blood of people and animals.

Under the killing ground

Under the floor were corridors and rooms. In these people and animals were kept before being sent up into the arena to die. These can still be seen because the wooden floor has rotted away.

Because the floor is no longer there today, you can look down into the corridors and rooms that were once below the arena. The pillars show where the wooden floor would once have rested on them. A sandy floor would have covered the whole area in Roman times.

A day of death

Before dawn, animals arrived for the day's events. Trained people, called 'bestiarii', got them into cages ready for the day. At 9 a.m., these same people hunted these animals to death. The animals included leopards and lions. In the middle of the morning, animals killed criminals tied to stakes. At noon, armed men hacked down crowds of unarmed people sentenced to death. At 2 p.m., the gladiators came on. People fought people to the death. Special workers dragged bodies out of the arena and spread sand over the blood.

These smooth marble walls were built to stop people, or animals, climbing out of the arena.

Historians used to think sea battles took place in the Colosseum too, because Roman writers say the arena was sometimes flooded. The triangular drains at the back of this picture were thought to show how water from a 'sea battle' would have been removed from the Colosseum. But historians now think the 'sea battles' took place elsewhere and that these drains just kept the arena dry.

21

Gladiators in the arena

A gladiator is a person who fights other people to entertain a crowd, in a savage human blood-sport. The first gladiators were slaves who fought to the death at the funerals of wealthy Romans. They were **sacrifices** meant to please the spirits of the dead. To impress more people some of these fights were held at first in the Forum. Julius Caesar held gladiator games in memory of his dead daughter. This meant he did not have to wait for a funeral to put on fights to the death. Soon rich Romans were competing for who could put on the biggest number of gladiators to entertain the Roman people and win support. The first **Emperor**, Augustus put on shows involving a total of 10,000 gladiators during his 40 years as emperor.

This large gateway (above) faces west. Written evidence from Roman times tells us that the western gate was used by gladiators to enter the arena.

Opposite the great western gate, is the eastern gateway. Slaves with carts dragged away the dead bodies of people and animals through it. These slaves were often dressed as Charon, Roman god of the dead.

The Colosseum had the biggest gladiator fights in the whole Roman **Empire**. In AD 107, Emperor Trajan had 10,000 gladiators fight there in just one set of games over a few days! Most gladiators at the Colosseum were men, but some were women. Female gladiators were finally banned in AD 200. At times dwarves were made to fight to the death and sometimes blind people were made to fight each other. This was thought to be a comedy event.

This is one of 24 little rooms, which were in a narrow passageway between the arena and the first seats. Drains show that some of these were used as toilets. One wall and the roof of the passage are no longer there, so the rooms can now be seen from the arena.

Looking down through what used to be the floor of the Colosseum it is possible to see the little rooms in which gladiators got ready for the killing.

Animals in the arena

The Colosseum told the world how great Rome was. **Emperors** were keen to bring animals to it from all over the Roman **Empire**. As well as entertaining the crowds, the range of animals showed how big and varied the empire was. They showed how 'civilized' Romans were the masters of the 'uncivilized' natural world of animals. Special animal keepers (called 'bestiarii') were trained to deal with wild animals from all over the Roman Empire.

The animals included lions, leopards, elephants, crocodiles, bulls, ostriches, hippos and deer. When the Colosseum was opened in AD 80, 5000 animals were killed in the first one hundred days. Many more died between then and the very last animal hunt in AD 523.

These corridors (right) were made very narrow, so that animals being driven into the arena could not turn around and bite the bestiarii.

These rooms are at the lowest level under the arena floor. This is where animals were kept.

Animals were set against other animals. Hunters, called 'venatores', fought animals and hills were built and trees were planted in the arena to make the animal hunts look more natural. Animals were used to tear apart people sentenced to death. As well as criminals, Christians were fed to wild animals because they would not worship the gods of Rome.

A zoo of death

In the ruins of the Colosseum, the places used to keep the thousands of animals can still be seen. Small rooms were used as cages. Narrow corridors helped keepers to control the animals. Lifts carried animals up to the floor below the arena. Trap doors opened and animals ran up ramps and out into the daylight. The animals were often frightened of the people they were supposed to kill, so their victims were splashed with blood, as the smell of blood made the animals more savage and willing to attack. Around the arena was a platform from which archers could fire arrows to kill any animal which became out of control.

The grooves in the walls, either side of the narrow doorway, show where a lift slid, pulling a cage of animals up to the arena. There were 32 of these lifts in the Colosseum. The stone in front of the doorway, with a hole in the middle, once supported a wooden post which was part of the lift.

*O*n the terraces

ooking at the Colosseum today, the ruined arches still show where tiers of seats rose high up above the arena. These were the terraces on which 50,000 people sat. To get this amount of people in, round, bone tickets were used – like at a modern sports event. The tickets showed the level and seat number. This made it easy to find a seat.

Front row seats for the rich

The richest people (Senators and the male members of their families) were allowed to sit on the lowest level of seats. This meant they were closest to the arena and the 'action'. Powerful Senators even had their names carved on their seats. Behind them sat wealthier Romans. Poorer Romans sat on higher levels. They sat on wooden benches. At the top level were slaves and women. The Vestal **Virgins** were the only women allowed close to the arena.

This seat must have belonged to a Senator because only such powerful people were allowed to have their names carved on their seats.

These ring-side stone seats could only be used by the most powerful **citizens**. They show how close to the killing they wanted to be.

These under-floor corridors – called 'vomitoria' in Latin – explain how 50,000 people could get in, or out, in under 15 minutes. Some people think it could have been done in as little as 5 minutes!

No trouble on the terraces

In over 300 years of use there is no record of a single riot in the Colosseum. Ramps and corridors under the seating levels made it easy to get in and out. This stopped people pushing and shoving. It also meant soldiers could get in quickly if anyone started causing trouble. And most Romans enjoyed the show too much to cause much trouble.

The remains of the **Emperor**'s seat show how he wanted to be as close as possible to the action. One Emperor, Commodus (ruled from AD 180 to 192), even fought in the arena.

With the fall of the Roman **Empire** the Forum and Colosseum gradually stopped being used. The marble was taken away for use in other buildings. Cows grazed in the Forum. In the 18th century, the Pope stopped the destruction of the Colosseum. In the 19th century, excavations uncovered what had survived in the Forum.

This water trough, from which people could get a drink, reminds us that everything was done to make the crowd's visit to the Colosseum a happy one. There were even fountains spraying perfume and fires burning **incense** to cover the smell of blood.

These carefully made brick walls, columns and arches show how different levels of seats were raised up like those in a modern sports stadium.

*T*imeline

8th century BC	Villages on the hills beside the River Tiber begin to come together to form the town – later city – of Rome
7th century BC	Marshy land in the valley between the hills is drained and paved to make the Forum Romanum (Roman Forum), the centre of Rome
497 BC	Temple of Saturn built in the Forum. Later rebuilt several times.
484 BC	Temple of Castor and Pollux built in the Forum. Later rebuilt several times.
338 BC	Rostra built in the Forum
184 BC	Earliest basilica – the Basilica Porcia – built in the Forum by the wealthy Roman, Marcus Porcius Cato
179 BC	Basilica Aemilia built in the Forum
78 BC	Tabularium record house built
54 BC	Julius Caesar starts the building of the Basilica Julia in the Forum
44 BC	Curia Julia built in the Forum as a place for the Senate to meet
29 BC	Temple of Julius Caesar built in the Forum by Augustus, the first **emperor** and Caesar's adopted **heir**
AD 64	St Peter may have been kept in Tullianum prison before his execution
AD 70	Vespasian starts work on the Colosseum
AD 80	Colosseum opens
AD 82	Building work completed on the Colosseum
AD 107	Emperor Trajan has 10,000 gladiators fight in one set of games
AD 110	First Christian killed in the Colosseum
AD 141	Temple of Antoninus (and his wife Faustina) built in the Forum
AD 200	Women gladiators banned from fighting in the Colosseum
AD 203	Arch of Emperor Septimius Severus built in the Forum to celebrate his victories in the Middle East
AD 230	Emperor Alexander Severus adds fourth storey to Colosseum
AD 300	Curia Julia rebuilt after a fire destroyed it in AD 283
AD 313	Basilica of Constantine opens in the Forum
AD 395	The Christian Emperor Theodosius orders the Temple of Vesta shut and the Vestal fire put out
Late 4th century AD	As the Roman **Empire** declined it became too difficult to put on expensive Colosseum games. Also the Christian Church opposed the killing. The Colosseum declined.
AD 404	Christian Emperor Honorius stops gladiator games
AD 410	Rome captured by **barbarian Goths**. Basilica Aemilia burnt down.
AD 438	Christian Emperor Valentinian bans gladiator games forever
AD 523	Last animal hunt held in the Colosseum

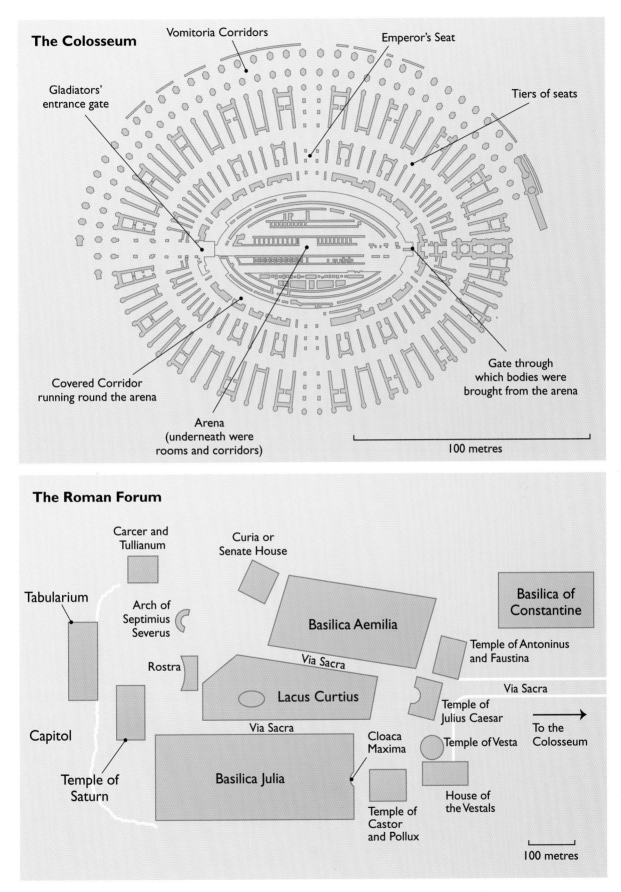

The Colosseum

Vomitoria Corridors

Emperor's Seat

Gladiators' entrance gate

Tiers of seats

Covered Corridor running round the arena

Gate through which bodies were brought from the arena

Arena (underneath were rooms and corridors)

100 metres

The Roman Forum

Carcer and Tullianum

Curia or Senate House

Tabularium

Basilica of Constantine

Arch of Septimius Severus

Basilica Aemilia

Temple of Antoninus and Faustina

Rostra

Via Sacra

Via Sacra

Lacus Curtius

Capitol

Temple of Julius Caesar

To the Colosseum

Via Sacra

Cloaca Maxima

Temple of Vesta

Basilica Julia

Temple of Saturn

Temple of Castor and Pollux

House of the Vestals

100 metres

Glossary

awning cover to keep off the sun. The one hoisted over the Colosseum was made of silk and hauled into place by Roman sailors.

barbarian word used in the Roman Empire to describe tribes living outside the Empire

citizen person with rights and responsibilities in Rome

cremate burn a dead body to ashes

emperor ruler of an empire. Rome had its first Emperor – one man in charge of all Roman land – in 27 BC. But it had been conquering neighbouring peoples and building an empire since the 3rd century BC.

empire collection of countries and people conquered and ruled by another country

Gauls tribes living in what is now France. Julius Caesar conquered them.

Goths Germanic people who invaded the Roman Empire

heir someone who receives money, or power, left to them by a person who has died

holy something special in a religion

incense something burnt to make a nice smell

legend story which may have a small amount of truth in it

magistrate person running a Roman court and deciding what sentence should be given to a guilty person

politician person involved in government

prow front of a ship. In Roman times these were often pointed to ram and sink enemy ships.

public buildings places built by the government and used in the running of a city and country, or open for people to use

reconstruction modern building made to look how an old one once looked

republic country without a king, or queen. Rome was a republic between 509 BC when Romans drove out their last king and 27 BC when Octavian (called Augustus) became the first Emperor.

Sabine ancient people from central Italy

sacred special and holy

sacrifice kill animals as gifts to gods. The killing itself performed by a Roman priest.

sculptor person who carves in stone

sewer drain to take away water and waste

treaty agreement made between countries

vault strong room, under a building

virgin person who has not had sexual intercourse

will document in which a person says who should have their possessions after they die

*I*ndex

Titles in the *Visiting the past* series include:

Visiting the Past

Colosseum & Roman Forum

Martyn Whittock

Hardback   0 431 02786 2

Visiting the Past

The D-Day Landing Sites

Bob Rees

Hardback   0 431 02787 0

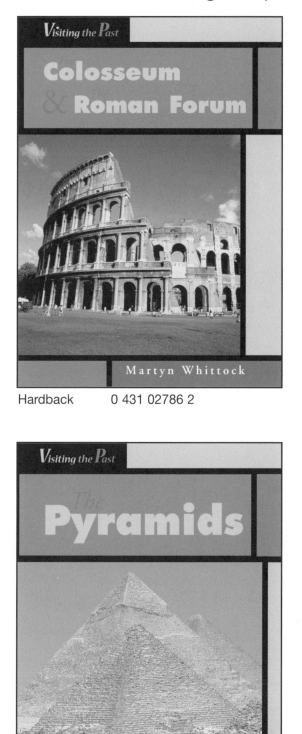

Visiting the Past

The Pyramids

Haydn Middleton

Hardback   0 431 02784 6

Visiting the Past

Shakespeare's Birthplace

Jane Shuter

Hardback   0 431 02785 4

Find out about the other titles in this series on our website www.heinemann.co.uk/library